The Origin and Operation of

DEMONS

**Volume 1 of the Satan, Demons, and Demon
Possession Series**

By Kenneth E. Hagin

Second Edition
First Printing 1983

ISBN 0-89276-025-7

In the U.S. write:
Kenneth Hagin Ministries
P.O. Box 50126
Tulsa, Oklahoma 74150

In Canada write:
Kenneth Hagin Ministries
P.O. Box 335
Islington (Toronto), Ontario
Canada, M9A 4X3

FAITH LIBRARY

Contents

The Satan, Demons, and Demon Possession Series:

Volume 1 — *The Origin and Operation of Demons*
Volume 2 — *Demons and How To Deal With Them*
Volume 3 — *Ministering to the Oppressed*
Volume 4 — *Bible Answers to Man's Questions on Demons*

Foreword

The Book of Revelation teaches us, "...*for the devil is come down unto you, having great wrath, because he knoweth that he hath but a short time*" (Rev. 12:12).

This is the reason there is such an increase of demon activity the world around. The devil knows his time is short.

Yet, though demon activity has increased, knowledge in spiritual matters has increased. The Spirit of God said to me concerning this:

"There is coming what men call a breakthrough. In the spiritual realm it existed all the time. But in the natural realm a breakthrough is coming in the area of the spirit world and spirit activity — demonology, if you would like to call it that.

"Also, a breakthrough is coming in the realm of spirits concerning angels — for they are spirits. There is coming further revelation; there is coming what some men would call an explosion."

And I heard the Spirit of God say:

"I have brought men to this place before, but that move I desired, that revival, that flow, was miscarried, sometimes aborted.

"You see, abortion and miscarriage are not the same. Men can bring about abortion; miscarriage is from natural causes. So it was sometimes aborted, sometimes miscarried, and in other cases derailed by humans as they went their own way with it.

"But this time, because of the balance of the Word and the knowledge of the Word, this revival, this anointing, shall not be miscarried, shall not be aborted, shall not be derailed. But it shall come forth in great power and mighty force.

"Oh yes, there'll be some over on the fringes who'll mix their own ideas with it and create havoc and confusion. But the main body of those who understand and know the

things of the Spirit will walk down the middle of the road. And they'll be a blessing, and not a curse, and will bring help to humanity. And great shall be the deliverances thereof."

Kenneth E. Hagin

Tulsa, Oklahoma
July 1983

Chapter 1
The Origin of Demons

This is the first volume in a three-part series on the devil, demons, and demon activity. This book will deal with the origin and fall of Satan or Lucifer.

How did Satan originate? Is it possible he once ruled a kingdom in the earth?

Satan's Earthly Kingdom

Ephesians 6:12 says, *"For we wrestle not against flesh and blood, but against principalities, against powers, against the rulers of the darkness of this world, against spiritual wickedness in high places."* A marginal note in my *King James Version* says, "wicked spirits in the heavenlies."

Three heavens are spoken of in the Bible. Scholars agree that the Apostle Paul was talking about himself in Second Corinthians 12:2 when he said, *"I knew a man in Christ above fourteen years ago, (whether in the body, I cannot tell; or whether out of the body, I cannot tell: God knoweth;) such an one caught up to the third heaven."*

The first of the three heavens, right above us, is what we call the atmospheric heaven. Beyond that, out in space, are the stars. Out beyond that is the third heaven — the heaven of heavens — where the throne of God is.

There *are* wicked spirits in the atmospheric heaven above us — "in the heavenlies." We get another glimpse of this fact in the 28th chapter of Ezekiel.

EZEKIEL 28:1-10
1 The word of the Lord came again unto me, saying,
2 Son of man, say unto the prince of Tyrus, Thus saith the Lord God; Because thine heart is lifted up, and thou hast said, I am a God, I sit in the seat of God, in the midst of the seas; yet thou art a man, and not God, though thou

set thine heart as the heart of God:

3   Behold, thou art wiser than Daniel; there is no secret that they can hide from thee:

4   With thy wisdom and with thine understanding thou hast gotten thee riches, and hast gotten gold and silver into thy treasures:

5   By thy great wisdom and by thy traffick hast thou increased thy riches, and thine heart is lifted up because of thy riches:

6   Therefore thus saith the Lord God; Because thou hast set thine heart as the heart of God;

7   Behold, therefore I will bring strangers upon thee, the terrible of the nations: and they shall draw their swords against the beauty of thy wisdom, and they shall defile thy brightness.

8   They shall bring thee down to the pit, and thou shalt die the deaths of them that are slain in the midst of the seas.

9   Wilt thou yet say before him that slayeth thee, I am God? but thou shalt be a man, and no God, in the hand of him that slayeth thee.

10 Thou shalt die the deaths of the uncircumcised by the hand of strangers: for I have spoken it, saith the Lord God.

This Scripture is a prophetic message, given through the prophet Ezekiel to the prince of Tyrus, who was lifted up in pride. God said, *"yet thou art a man."* So this prince of Tyrus was a man. Angels are not men. Evil spirits are not men.

In verses 11-19 of that same chapter, another prophetic word is given through Ezekiel, but this one is addressed to the *king* of Tyrus, a being who could not be the *prince* of Tyrus, whom God had identified earlier as a man. The king of Tyrus, therefore, must be a spiritual power, or dark power, behind this kingdom.

EZEKIEL 28:11-19

11 Moreover the word of the Lord came unto me, saying,

12 Son of man, take up a lamentation upon the king of Tyrus, and say unto him, Thus saith the Lord God; Thou

sealest up the sum, full of wisdom, and perfect in beauty.
13 Thou hast been in Eden the garden of God; every
precious stone was thy covering, the sardius, topaz, and
the diamond, the beryl, the onyx, and the jasper, the sap-
phire, the emerald, and the carbuncle, and gold: the
workmanship of thy tabrets and of thy pipes was prepared
in thee in the day that thou wast created.
14 Thou art the anointed cherub that covereth; and I have
set thee so: thou wast upon the holy mountain of God; thou
hast walked up and down in the midst of the stones of fire.
15 Thou wast perfect in thy ways from the day that thou
wast created, till iniquity was found in thee.
16 By the multitude of thy merchandise they have filled
the midst of thee with violence and thou hast sinned:
therefore I will cast thee as profane out of the mountain
of God: and I will destroy thee, O covering cherub, from
the midst of the stones of fire.
17 Thine heart was lifted up because of thy beauty, thou
hast corrupted thy wisdom by reason of thy brightness:
I will cast thee to the ground, I will lay thee before kings,
that they may behold thee.
18 Thou hast defiled thy sanctuaries by the multitude of
thine iniquities, by the iniquity of thy traffick; therefore
will I bring forth a fire from the midst of thee, it shall
devour thee, and I will bring thee to ashes upon the earth
in the sight of all them that behold thee.
19 All they that know thee among the people shall be
astonished at thee: thou shalt be a terror, and never shalt
thou be any more.

God was talking about the devil — Lucifer — when He
said, *"Thou hast been in Eden the garden of God...."*
The prince of Tyrus, a man, couldn't have been there. He
hadn't even been born then. No, this "king of Tyrus" is
not a man; he is a created being (vv. 13,15).

In these two beings — the prince of Tyrus, a man; and
the king of Tyrus, a spirit being (Lucifer himself) — the
Bible gives the idea of a natural kingdom upon the earth
dominated by a spiritual kingdom with the same name.

Everything on this earth — every human, every being

— is dominated, ruled, or influenced by the unseen world. Where did these spirits come from originally? First of all, the devil and demons are fallen beings. Satan, or Lucifer, as we read, *"wast perfect in all thy ways from the day that thou wast created"* (Ezek. 28:15). The Bible is talking about a created being, not a human being. But God didn't create him as he is now.

The second part of Ezekiel 28:15 tells us iniquity was found in him. Isaiah tells us, *"For thou hast said in thine heart, I will ascend into heaven, I will exalt my throne above the stars of God: I will sit also upon the mount of the congregation, in the sides of the north"* (Isa. 14:13). This is when he sinned. He said, *"I will ascend above the heights of the clouds; I will be like the most High"* (Isa. 14:14).

Scientists tell us there is a vacant spot in the North they have been unable to probe. That is the "sides of the north" where the throne of God is. Apparently Lucifer had some kind of throne, because he said, *"I will exalt my throne above the stars of God."* And apparently he was under the clouds, because he said, *"I will ascend above the heights of the clouds."* So Satan had some kind of kingdom on earth. This would lead us to believe in a "pre-Adamic" creation. Evidently there was some kind of kingdom on earth before man was created.

The Pre-Adamic Race

Many Bible scholars believe that millions of years may have elapsed between Genesis 1:1 and Genesis 1:2. Genesis 1:2 tells us, *"And the earth was without form, and void; and darkness was upon the face of the deep. And the Spirit of God moved upon the face of the waters."*

Evidently the spirits that are here on earth now were part of that original kingdom. Remember, God told Adam and Eve to be fruitful and multiply and to replenish the earth. He didn't say "plenish." You can't *re*plenish something that hasn't already been plenished.

God said the same thing to Noah, his wife, his three sons, and their wives. It is certainly true that we have the same animals this side of the flood that we had on the other side of it.

Yet we know from archeological discoveries that dinosaurs and other types of animals existed. Where did they come from? They didn't come from our system, so it looks like there had to be a different kind of creation here before Adam.

Satan, or Lucifer, had a kingdom here evidently. Now, I don't have chapter and verse for what I'm saying. But evil spirits *are* here on the earth. Where did they come from? To me, the only logical explanation would be that they are the spirits of this pre-Adamic creation. I didn't say *man* was here before. But some kind of creation could have been.

I'm not presenting this dogmatically, because we don't have enough light on this from the Scriptures to be dogmatic. But we do get a glimpse here and there.

Here's another interesting thing concerning the origin and fall of Lucifer. Ezekiel 28:13 tells us, "...*the workmanship of thy tabrets and of thy pipes was prepared in thee in the day that thou wast created.*"

Evidently Lucifer had something to do with music. Did you ever notice how music has always played a part in the program of God, as well as that of Satan? When David played on his harp it quieted that evil spirit in Saul. The right kind of music prepares you to yield to the Spirit of God, while the wrong kind will prepare you to yield to the spirit of the devil. The devil works through the flesh, while God works through your spirit.

God's Original Creation

At least Isaiah 14 and Ezekiel 28 give us a picture of the fall of Satan and of his existence in the beginning. We have said God didn't make him as he is today. God made everything in the beginning and it was all good.

There are philosophers who are so taken up with the evil in the world they have supposed the center of the universe is evil instead of good. Some people have accused God of being the author and creator of evil.

I read an article some time ago written by a well-known newspaper man here in America. He wrote that he was not religiously inclined, didn't belong to any church, and never had. He did not believe the Bible was the Word of God; he didn't believe God existed.

He said, "I wouldn't exactly say I'm an atheist; an atheist says there is no God. Perhaps I would be called an agnostic. An agnostic says, 'If there is a God, I don't know it.'

"Christians say," he continued, "that God is running this universe, and that there is a God who created everything.

"And," he said, "it's here, and logically speaking it would seem someone did create it.

"But," he continued, "here is my point. They say God is the ruler of this universe and He's running everything. If He is, He surely has things in a mess. Why doesn't He put a stop to war and poverty and innocent babies dying?"

He was saying if God is a good God and is ruling, why doesn't He do something about these things? He had only heard one side of the argument. If he ever had heard the Bible preached, he would have known that God made the world in the beginning and saw that everything was good. He made man and gave him dominion over the work of His hands, but Satan came into the Garden, tempted Eve,

and she ate the forbidden fruit. She gave it to Adam and
he ate. Adam committed high treason and sold out to the
devil. Then the devil became the god of this world (2 Cor.
4:4).

Thank God, He set out a plan of redemption for us, and
those of us who have accepted that plan are redeemed from
the hand of the enemy. But those who are unsaved are
dominated and ruled by the devil, not by God.

Demons in Certain Regions

Demons and evil spirits want to possess man so they
can find the widest range of expression in this world. If
they can't find embodiment in man, they'll take embodiment in animals as a second choice. The spirits in the fifth
chapter of Mark said they wanted to go into the swine so
they wouldn't have to go out of the country. Jesus gave
them permission and they went into the swine.

> **MARK 5:9-12**
> 9 And he asked him, What is thy name? And he answered,
> saying, My name is Legion: for we are many.
> 10 And he besought him much that he would not send them
> away out of the country.
> 11 Now there was there nigh unto the mountains a great
> herd of swine feeding.
> 12 And all the devils besought him, saying, Send us into
> the swine, that we may enter into them.

We see from this Scripture that demons do like to gang
up in certain parts of the world or certain countries.

In traveling, it has been easy for me to discern what
kinds of spirits are in a locality. I can drive through a city
and know what spirits predominate there. Sometimes there
are immoral or occult spirits, or spirits promoting foreign
religions. Small towns — not just large cities — can have
spirits ruling over them, too.

Spirits in the Church

My wife and I were in a town visiting her relatives one time, and the pastor of the church there said he wanted me to preach. I was on the field in evangelism, and he kept asking me. Finally I told him I wasn't going to do it. He asked me if there were something wrong with him and his wife. I told him there wasn't. But I explained I didn't want to preach in that town unless God definitely told me to. I told him the town was full of reserved, conservative people, motivated by stingy devils and demons. I told him these demons had gotten into his church and that the people wouldn't support me if I went there.

His eyes got big and his mouth fell open, and he asked me if anyone had been talking to me. I told him no one but the Lord.

Whatever kinds of spirits are in a city will get into the church, because there will be someone who will let them in. For instance, look at the Church at Corinth. Corinth was one of the most immoral cities of the East. This immoral devil got into the church. There was a man cohabiting with his father's wife. It had to be dealt with.

First Corinthians 5:1 tells us, *"It is reported commonly that there is fornication among you, and such fornication as is not so much as named among the Gentiles, that one should have his father's wife."*

Whatever spirits are predominant in a city will get into the church unless individuals and the church as a whole learn to stand against them.

This minister decided to tell me some things. He said he had taken that church without promise of any set salary. Whatever came in as tithes and offerings on Sunday morning was to be his. The Sunday night and Wednesday night offerings would go for payments on the church building and utilities.

When he first came, he didn't have enough money to get by on. But he believed God and sacrificed, and the church started growing. He had been getting about $80 a week, but he began getting around $200, which in that day was a large amount.

At this time the board had a meeting without him and decided, "That's just too much. Let's use some of this money for improvements on the building. Whatever is left over we'll give to him."

The Bible says, "...*Thou shalt not muzzle the ox that treadeth out the corn. And, The labourer is worthy of his reward*" (1 Tim. 5:18). Paul said that, and he's quoting the Old Testament, talking about the ministry. In one sense, this church was stealing the pastor's money!

I told him, "That's why I won't come." Unless God tells you to, there's no use going to a group like that. *They can't be blessed too much anyway.* They are motivated by evil spirits.

When Jesus was talking about going to the cross and dying, Peter took hold of Him and said, "*Be it far from thee, Lord: this shall not be unto thee.*" Jesus said, "*Get thee behind me, Satan: thou art an offence unto me: for thou savourest not the things that be of God, but those that be of men.*" He wasn't calling Peter Satan, but He knew Peter unconsciously was yielding to the devil.

The board in that church didn't yield *unconsciously* to the devil. They had the new plan down in writing. That's just being crooked. People wonder why God isn't in some churches and isn't blessing them. He can't bless people like that. It won't work.

One time I traveled to hold a meeting in another state. When I drove up to the parsonage, the pastor said he had something he wanted to tell me. He said he was leaving that church and taking another one. He added, however, that we would go right on with the meeting, as he was supposed to be there 30 more days. He was a good pastor and his people loved him, but they were so spiritually dead. After one service I told him I wasn't going to have a revival there. I told him I was leaving.

The next day his brother came over and asked me where I was going. (I had about three free weeks.) He invited me to come to preach at his church, so I told him I would. When I got there he told me his church wasn't as large as his brother's and that they couldn't support me as well. His board felt $70 or $80 a week was the most they could give me. I needed about $150 to meet my budget, so they decided to take up an offering for me every night except Monday.

On Tuesday night of the second week, the Spirit of God suddenly came upon me and I ran off the platform and sat down beside a man. I looked him right in the face and told him some people were trying to steal my money. I said if it came in for me, it belonged to me. I then ran back to the platform and finished my sermon.

The pastor later told me the man I talked to had told the church board too much money had come in for me. He had suggested they keep half of it. The Holy Spirit told on him, because I noticed when I spoke to him he turned every color but white. If I had known what he had done, I wouldn't have had enough nerve to say that to him. It was a wrong spirit that he had. I believe the man was saved and had the baptism in the Holy Spirit, but I don't believe he yielded *unconsciously* to the devil. He knew what he was doing. These spirits are here on earth.

Paul said in Ephesians 6:12, *"For we wrestle not against flesh and blood, but against principalities, against powers, against the rulers of darkness of this world, against spiritual wickedness in high places."* It wasn't just the man who had to be dealt with; it was the spirit behind the man. That kind of spirit controlling the church will give the devil a right-of-way. It will hinder and grieve the Spirit of God. We must realize we don't have to listen to the devil.

Spiritual and Physical Health

A minister once told about a missionary who was going to speak in his church. He met the man at a railroad station after not seeing him for several years. They hadn't been in the car five minutes when the missionary said, "You're not 'up to par' spiritually."

The pastor didn't say too much about it, but when he was alone he talked to the Lord. It seems there had been just one Full Gospel church in that town when another pastor came in and started one also. That pastor had taken some of this first pastor's members. So the first pastor had gone around telling that the other minister had stolen some of his sheep, though he didn't know it for sure. It had gotten him down.

He finally went to the new preacher's house, fell down crying, and asked him to forgive him and pray for him. He told him what he had done. The new preacher started crying also and asked this pastor to forgive him, because he *had* been working on some of his people. They got to hugging one another, crying and praying until they got in line spiritually. God blessed both of their churches. The first pastor doubled what he had been running.

It's quite obvious at times that we're under a load. Sometimes we're carrying a chip on our shoulder. That's wrong. Through that we open the door and let a wrong spirit get hold of us. It doesn't mean we're not saved, but it means we're yielding to the wrong spirit. Let's be big enough, like this pastor was, to admit when we're wrong. Paul told the Church at Ephesus they shouldn't give place to the devil.

Chapter 2
The Operation of Demons

I was conducting a two-week meeting in Oklahoma years ago, and one night after the service the pastor and I were visiting and having sandwiches in his kitchen. We became engaged discussing Scriptures and it was getting late. Finally the pastor's little daughter reminded him it was time to pray with her.

He started to get up but then said, "Honey, come back and kneel down here. We'll get Brother Hagin to pray with us. Then you can go to bed." They both knelt beside my chair and I joined them.

I no more expected anything unusual to happen at that moment than I expected to be the first man to land on the moon. I never felt so ordinary in my life. But when I knelt, a white cloud enveloped me. I couldn't see a thing. My eyes were wide open, but I couldn't see the stove, the table, or anything in the kitchen. Many times in the Old Testament the glory of God manifested in a cloud.

I looked up where the ceiling should have been, and saw Jesus standing there. He spent an hour and a half talking to me, and He began His conversation by saying, "I'm going to talk to you about the devil, demons, and demon possession. From this night forward, what is known in my Word as discerning of spirits will operate in your life when you're in the Spirit."

Now, John was in the Spirit on the Lord's Day on the Isle of Patmos. He saw some things. And when Peter went up on the housetop to pray, he fell into a trance. He saw a great sheet let down from heaven. Paul said when he went to the Temple in Jerusalem to pray, he went into a trance and saw Jesus. The Lord told him people would not accept his testimony there.

Your physical senses are suspended when you fall into a trance. It seems you're in another world. You *are* in the spirit world. And the spirit world is just as real as the material world — in fact, more real. God, who is a Spirit, created all material things.

The pastor and his daughter didn't see anything, but I was seeing into the spirit realm by the power of the Holy Spirit. Now, a person doesn't operate something from God whenever he wants to. I wasn't operating that gift. Jesus said, "The gift will operate when you're in the Spirit."

People get in trouble trying to operate in spiritual gifts when they're not in the Spirit. I would suggest that you do not even become interested in the gifts of the Spirit unless you purpose to live and walk in the Spirit.

Many times I've prayed for people and never had any manifestation of discerning of spirits. Then, at a later date, a manifestation comes, and I'm able to deal with the spirit. With other people, I never do have a manifestation.

We need to preach faith and preach the Word of God to get people to believe God. *Then* we need to expect God to manifest Himself through the gifts of the Holy Spirit as He wills. First Corinthians 12:7 tells us: *"But the manifestation of the Spirit is given to every man to profit withal."* The manifestation is given as the Spirit wills — not as *I* will.

Discerning of Devils?

Jesus talked to me for some time about discerning of spirits: supernatural insight into the realm of spirits. People who claim to have this gift and who see only devils or demons, don't have what the Bible describes. The Bible doesn't say "discerning of devils," but "discerning of spirits." Another thing — the gift of discerning of spirits (1 Cor. 12:10) has to do with spirits — not people. People can be motivated by spirits. But the gift still has to do with the spirit and not the person.

In Acts 16, Paul and Silas were at Philippi, where there was a maiden with a spirit of divination or fortune telling. She followed them on the street saying they were servants of the Most High God. Everything she said was true. But who wants the devil testifying for him?

I'm sure Paul didn't carry discerning of spirits around with him and turn it off and on whenever he wanted to. This girl followed him a number of days before he dealt with the situation. It's my conviction he didn't deal with it sooner because the Spirit didn't give him discerning of spirits. When the Lord did operate that gift through him, Paul turned and spoke to the evil spirit, not the woman. The spirit came out of her and she was delivered. The devil never likes it when God is moving. Her masters got mad about it and had Paul and Silas put in jail.

Many times people have told me the Lord gave them a "gift of *discernment*." In the first place, there isn't such a gift spoken of in the Bible. Sometimes these people are talking about the gift of the word of knowledge. But most of the time, if you'll talk to them, you'll find the "gift" they have is only a "gift of suspicion." They are suspicious of everybody.

In the realm of the Spirit there are good spirits as well as bad spirits. If you have discerning of spirits operating, you're going to see angels sometimes as well as demons.

In Second Kings, chapter 6, it is recorded that the king of Syria warred against Israel. At one time Syria besieged the city of Dothan. The Syrians were really after Elisha, the prophet of God, who divulged secrets of the king of Syria to the king of Israel. When the Syrian army had surrounded the city, Elisha's servant was fearful and asked Elisha what they were going to do.

The prophet asked the Lord to open the servant's eyes. He was talking about his spiritual eyes. Verse 17 tells us: "*And the Lord opened the eyes of the young man; and he saw: and, behold, the mountain was full of horses and chariots of fire round about Elisha."* He was seeing into the realm of the Spirit. He was seeing supernaturally.

Four Classes of Demons

After Jesus finished talking to me about discerning of spirits, he reminded me Paul stated in Ephesians 6:12 that we *"wrestle not against flesh and blood, but against principalities, against powers, against the rulers of the darkness of this world, against spiritual wickedness in high places."*

Jesus said there were four classes of demons or evil spirits: (1) principalities, (2) powers, (3) rulers of the darkness of this world, and (4) wicked spirits in the heavenlies. He explained the highest type of demon we have to deal with on earth is "rulers of the darkness of this world." He spent some time talking to me about the fact that the Bible says the whole world lies in darkness.

The Bible tells us, though, in Colossians 1:13, that the Father has delivered us from the rulers of darkness: *"Who hath delivered us from the power of darkness, and hath translated us into the kingdom of his dear Son."*

Paul was writing to the Church at Corinth when he said, *"Be ye not unequally yoked together with unbelievers: for what fellowship hath righteousness with unrighteousness? and what communion hath light with darkness?"* (2 Cor. 6:14). The unbelievers are called darkness and the believers are called light.

The Lord went on to tell me that all unsaved men and women, regardless of who they are, are in the kingdom of darkness. *He said they are ruled or motivated by evil spirits, whether they want to admit it or not.* It is easy, sometimes, to accept the fact that someone else is ruled by the devil. But it's hard to admit it could happen to us.

Jesus said this is the reason a person might do something his family members would say he'd never do, but he'd do that or something worse.

Jesus told me these rulers of darkness are the most intelligent type of spirits. They rule over other spirits and tell them what to do. Besides dominating the unsaved, they dominate Christians who will walk in darkness. He told me he would show me how these spirits get hold of people. He said sometimes they finally possess people — even children of God, if they will let them.

Paul wrote to the Church at Ephesus and said, *"Neither give place to the devil."* That means not to give the devil any place in you. If he does have a place in you, it's because *you* let him in.

How Possession Works

In the vision that night I saw a woman I had met one time. I immediately recognized her because I had heard her sing at a convention. She was the wife of a minister I knew. I saw her like you would see a picture on television.

Jesus narrated the story that followed. He said this woman was his servant. She'd had a part in the ministry, but then the devil came. I saw an evil spirit. It seemed to sit on her right shoulder and whisper in her ear. She *was* a Christian and the devil wasn't on the inside of her; he was on the outside. (But he'll work from the outside and try to get inside.)

As Jesus narrated this story, he said this demon told the woman she was beautiful, but that she had been cheated in life. He told her she could have had fame, fortune, and popularity in the world.

Jesus said the woman knew this was the devil, and told Satan to get behind her. He said the spirit left for a season. I saw it run off and leave her. But after a time it came back again and whispered into her ear that she was a beautiful woman. The devil told her again that in the world she could have had fame, popularity, and wealth.

Jesus said she began to entertain Satan's suggestion. We can learn something important here. *The only way the devil can get into you is through your mind. Your mind is the door to your spirit.* One of Satan's greatest weapons is suggestion.

Didn't the devil *suggest* to Eve that the reason God didn't want her to eat the forbidden fruit was because her eyes would be opened and she would become like God? She followed his suggestion. Jesus told me this woman began to entertain the suggestion that she was beautiful. She liked to think she was beautiful. (The Bible tells us in Ezekiel concerning the fall of Satan that he was lifted up in pride because of his beauty.) She felt she had been cheated in life. She felt she had been robbed. She felt in the world she could have had fame and fortune.

As I said, she was very outstanding. I had heard her sing at church conventions. She had whatever the world calls "it." If she came in late for a service, men and women alike couldn't keep from looking at her. She just had that "something" about her.

In the vision, she suddenly became like glass — transparent. And I could see something in her head that looked like a black dot. It was about as big as a half dollar. Jesus, in narrating, said, "She is now obsessed with that kind of thinking. But," He said, "it isn't too late — she still could do something about it."

We're supposed to think God's thoughts. That woman was still God's child. She could have put that thought out of her mind if she had wanted to. She could have refused to think like that. But she desired to think like that, so she continued. Somebody said, "You can't help who may knock on your front door, but you can help who you invite into the living room and entertain." *Thoughts may come and go, but thoughts that are not put into actions or words will die unborn.*

You may say, "I can't control my thoughts." Yes, you can unless the devil has taken over your spirit. Jesus told me this woman could have said from her spirit, "I'm not going to think like that. I resist you, Satan. I rebuke you in the Name of Jesus. Leave me!"

You see, if the devil is going to get into your spirit, he's going to have to come through your mind. I am referring to believers. You can cast devils out of people without teaching them and still do them an injustice. A lot of times they don't need a spirit cast out. They just need to rise up against it. And, like Jesus said, this woman could have done it.

The Bible tells us to cast down imaginations or reasonings. It tells us to cast down those things that exalt themselves against the knowledge of God, and to bring into captivity every thought to the obedience of Christ (2 Cor. 10:5).

Did He tell us to do something we can't do? No, thank God, He didn't. Now, quit saying, "I can't." As long as you talk unbelief, you're going to be bound by unbelief.

This woman soon left her husband and the ministry. She went out into the world. I asked the Lord why He was showing me this. He said it was because He didn't want me to pray for the woman. Also, He wanted me to know how demons and evil spirits get hold of people, even Christians if they will permit them to.

I asked Him if He wanted me to cast the devil out of this woman. She had left her husband and taken up with several different men at once. She wasn't satisfied with one man. Jesus told me this thing finally got down into her spirit. It got into her heart. I saw the black dot go from her head down into the inside of her. She began to say she didn't want the Lord Jesus anymore. She turned her back on Him. Before, she hadn't completely turned her back on Him.

The Lord told me she could have this devil if she wanted it. He told me no one, not even Himself when He was on earth, exercised authority over human spirits. God Himself does not exercise authority over human spirits. Jesus did exercise authority over evil spirits and demons, and any believer in the Church can do that. But if a *human spirit* wants the condition to remain as it is, there is nothing another believer can do about it.

I asked the Lord if He wanted me to pray for her. But He told me then not to even pray. That came as a real jolt to me. I'd never heard of not praying for people!

I'm one who is a stickler for the Word of God, so I asked the Lord if this was scriptural. He told me to look at First John 5:16, which says, "*If any man see his brother sin a sin which is not unto death, he shall ask, and he shall give him life for them that sin not unto death. There is a sin unto death: I do not say that he shall pray for it.*" I never had heard anyone preach on this before. But some eight years before, I'd had an unusual experience with this verse of Scripture.

I had stopped to see my mother and she'd told me I should visit my grandmother, who was very ill. I did stop to see her, but I was in a hurry. I wished afterwards I'd had a word of prayer with her.

Praying for Forgiveness

While I was at my next meeting I learned Granny had become unconscious. After preaching every night, I would go where she was, which was about 35 miles away, and stay up all night with her. The rest of the family would stay with her in the daytime. She was unconscious all the time, so there wasn't much to do except watch her in case she did wake up.

One night I was sitting in the large chair by her bed and began to pray. I said, "Lord, I wish I had prayed with Granny. I'm sorry I didn't have a word of prayer with her. I know she is 77 years of age — and I can sense in my spirit she has lived her life out — but if she could just regain consciousness and I could have a word of prayer with her . . . ."

I said, "I know she never would tell a lie for anything in the world." Yet, sometimes we can see sins of omission in our loved ones. I asked the Lord, "Let me have a word of prayer with her, so I can be sure everything is all right, and I will be willing to let her go." Sins of omission as well as sins of commission are wrong.

Granny had been born again in an old-time Methodist campmeeting in Tennessee when she was 14 years old. But for 40 years she'd had a serious physical condition — she couldn't hear out of her right ear. At one time she'd had an operation, but she still wasn't healed. The right side of her head always hurt, and as kids we never could jump around because she said it felt like something was pounding in her head. One time, however, some Full Gospel people laid hands on her and she was instantly healed.

Three years after that, when I was pastoring a church close by, I stopped and noticed she had cotton in her ear. I asked what was wrong and she said she had lost her healing. She had promised the Lord she would go to a church nearby, and would do more Bible reading and praying. But she hadn't done what she'd promised, so she had lost it.

I was thinking about these things and praying when a voice said, "Why don't you ask me to forgive her?" I was so startled I jumped out of my chair. My Bible and a book by A.B. Simpson went flying across the floor and back under the bed. I must have jumped three feet!

I looked, but nobody was behind my chair. I got down,

reached under the bed, and got my Bible and book. I sat back down and thought, *Well, this is the third night I have sat up with Granny, and my imagination is playing tricks on me.* I read a little while longer.

But then I got to thinking about this subject again. I said, "Lord, just bring her out of this coma and let me have a word of prayer with her so I can believe everything is confessed — and everything is all right. And I'll just let her go on home then."

Just as plain as if somebody were standing behind me, the voice said, "Why don't you ask Me to forgive her?" I jumped again. My Bible went flying one way and my book the other, all the way across the floor. I must have leaped three feet out of that chair again.

I picked up my book and looked behind the chair, but there wasn't anybody there. I said to myself, *I know I heard somebody say that!*

I went back into the next room, which was the kitchen. The door had been closed, so I looked behind the door. I looked all around. And I couldn't find anybody.

I went back to the bedroom where Momma was asleep, and I stood at the door and listened. I could tell by her breathing that she was sound asleep. I went back to another room where Grandpa was asleep in the back of the house, and I could tell by his breathing that he was sound asleep. Nobody else was in the house except the two of them.

I checked the back door. I even checked the screens and doors to make sure they were hooked or locked. I said to myself, *There couldn't have been anybody in here.* I went into the living room and looked behind the couch. I couldn't find anybody. I said to myself, *I know it sounded like a man's voice.*

I sat back down and decided, *Well, this is the third night I have been sitting up with Granny and she is nearly*

*dead. We expect her to die any minute. It's just my nerves.
It's just my imagination playing tricks on me.*

I read a little while longer, and then my mind got back
on Granny. I prayed for the third time, "Lord, I'm so sorry
— You forgive me — that I didn't pray with Granny. Just
let her come out of this coma and let me pray with her,
so I'll be sure everything is all right. Then I'll let her go
on home."

And the third time that voice said, "Why don't you
ask Me to forgive her?"

This time I didn't jump. I sat there and answered back,
"ME ask You to forgive her?"

And the voice said, "Yes. Did you ever read in First
John 5:16 where I said, *'If any man see his brother sin
a sin which is not unto death, he shall ask, and he shall
give him life for them that sin not unto death. There is
a sin unto death: I do not say that he shall pray for it'?*"

I told Him I still did not know what the verse meant.
He said He was referring to the first part of the verse and
He told me to ask Him to forgive Granny of every sin of
omission.

I did that, and also asked that she be forgiven of any
sins of commission. I asked that she be forgiven of every
wrong, fault, mistake, and failure. I asked that her
homecoming might be glorious. To me, that settled it.
There's nothing more sure than the Word of God. I didn't
build on an experience; the experience was built in line with
faith in God's Word.

Eight years later, when Jesus appeared to me in the
vision, He brought this verse up again. I told Him the only
time I'd had an encounter with it was the time I was with
Granny. He told me she had been in heaven with Him the
past eight years. But He told me the last part of this verse
says there is a sin unto death and that the Word says not
to pray for it.

The Sin Unto Death

He told me the reason I was not to pray for this preacher's wife was that she had sinned the sin unto death. I told the Lord I still wasn't satisfied with this. I wouldn't accept any kind of vision, or experience, even if I saw Jesus 20 times in one day, if what He said couldn't be proved by the written New Testament. I wouldn't accept a word of it. I told Him that His Word says, *"In the mouth of two or three witnesses every word may be established"* (Matt. 18:16). I asked Him for more Scripture and He gave me Hebrews 6:4-6.

> **HEBREWS 6:4-6**
> 4 For it is impossible for those who were once enlightened, and have tasted of the heavenly gift, and were made partakers of the Holy Ghost,
> 5 And have tasted the good word of God, and the powers of the world to come,
> 6 If they shall fall away, to renew them again unto repentance; seeing they crucify to themselves the Son of God afresh, and put him to an open shame.

Jesus said before one could be guilty of the sin unto death, all five things mentioned in that Scripture would have to apply to him.

First, it says, *"For it is impossible for those who were once enlightened."* He said that was what I had been calling "getting under conviction." The preaching of the Word enlightens the sinner, as in the case of the prodigal son when he came to himself. Through the preaching of God's Word the sinner sees himself lost.

Second, it says, *"and have tasted of the heavenly gift."* Jesus said a man under conviction has not yet tasted of the heavenly gift. You do not taste of the heavenly gift being under conviction, because Jesus said He is the heavenly gift. *"For God so loved the world, that he gave his only begotten Son, that whosoever believeth in him should not perish, but have everlasting life.*"

Then third, "*and were made partakers of the Holy Ghost.*" Jesus said that means more than becoming acquainted with the Holy Spirit and being born again; it means being filled with the Holy Spirit.

Then fourth, "*And have tasted the good word of God.*" He said this can't apply to baby Christians. They haven't tasted the good Word of God. First Peter 2:2 tells us: "*As newborn babes, desire the sincere milk of the word, that ye may grow thereby.*" Jesus said it was to be regretted that some believers act as they do. He pointed out the similarity between spiritual and physical growth. He said baby Christians can't be guilty of this sin. They wouldn't know what they were doing.

The fifth qualification is, "*And have tasted the powers of the world to come.*" Jesus interpreted this part as meaning, "And have the gifts of the Spirit operating in their lives." He said the baptism of the Holy Spirit with the ensuing gifts is the earnest of our inheritance in the world to come.

He told me this woman was enlightened, was born again, had tasted of the heavenly gift, was filled with the Holy Spirit, and had been in the ministry 20 years. She had experienced enough spiritual growth so that she wasn't a spiritual baby anymore. She had the gifts of the Spirit operating in her life.

Jesus said He would have forgiven her if she had just been tempted and overcome by the devil. He told me she didn't commit the sin unto death because she went off with another man. He explained if she'd had 100 men but turned back to Him He would have forgiven her. But Jesus told me she came to the place (without being tempted or overcome) that she *deliberately* said she didn't want Him anymore. That's what this sin is. Hebrews 10 explains it further.

HEBREWS 10:26-29
26 For if we sin wilfully after that we have received the
knowledge of the truth, there remaineth no more sacrifice
for sins,
27 But a certain fearful looking for of judgment and fiery
indignation, which shall devour the adversaries.
28 He that despised Moses' law died without mercy under
two or three witnesses.
29 Of how much sorer punishment, suppose ye, shall he
be thought worthy, who hath trodden under foot the Son
of God, and hath counted the blood of the covenant,
wherewith he was sanctified, an unholy thing, and hath
done despite unto the Spirit of grace?

Actually, this was written to Hebrew Christians. When
they accepted Christ as Savior they were cut off from the
rest of their families. The way was hard and they were
tempted to go back. If they went back to Judaism, they
had to deny Christ. If He is not the Son of God, then His
blood is unholy.

People have died at the stake because they wouldn't
recant. Now, if they recanted because pressure was put
on them, God wouldn't hold it against them. But if they
recanted willingly, that would make a difference. Jesus
said it was wrong and sinful that this woman had committed adultery, but He would have forgiven her. Yet she
had come to the place where she turned her back on the
Son of God and said she didn't want Him. She trod Him
underfoot.

I've had people come to me who think they've committed the unpardonable sin. I tell them that if they've never
turned their back on Jesus, they haven't committed this
sin. No matter what they've done, or how far away they've
wandered — even if they said some things against Jesus
in a moment of anger — He won't hold it against them.

I asked the Lord what would happen to this woman.
He said she would spend eternity in the lake of fire and

brimstone. In that vision I saw her go down into that place, and I heard her terrible screams.

Dealing With Spirits

I asked Jesus why He showed this to me. He said He did it for two reasons. First, He showed it to me because He wanted me to realize how demons and evil spirits can get hold of even *Christian* people. Second, the spirit in this woman's life was embarrassing, intimidating, and hindering her former husband. Jesus called her former husband His servant. He told me I couldn't deal with *her*, but that I could deal with that *spirit.* The woman's former husband had remarried. You can readily understand how the devil in that woman could cause him a lot of trouble.

The minister I am talking about is the one whose house I was in when I had the vision. I knew he had been married before, but I didn't know his first wife was phoning and threatening to come to his town. She could have caused a lot of trouble in the church and in the city.

Jesus told me to do something about this spirit. He told me to say, "You foul spirit that is operating and manifesting yourself in the life of So-and-so, I command you to desist in your maneuvers."

I asked the Lord if this was all I had to do. I thought perhaps I would have to prepare and get ready for it. But he told me this was all I had to do. I said it.

This pastor told me I did all my praying in tongues. He didn't know what I said or what I was dealing with, though I thought I was talking in English.

When I spoke to the demon, he answered me. Jesus told me I was beginning to see into the realm of spirits. The pastor didn't see or hear anything, but I both heard and saw.

The spirit said he sure didn't want to stop, but he knew

he had to if I told him to. He ran away like a whipped dog, and when he did, I started laughing. You can laugh in the Spirit.

Then I became tuned back to this earth and realized the pastor was laughing along with me. I don't know how long we laughed. After it was over, he asked me what I was laughing about. I told him I was lost in the spirit realm, but thought I had heard him laughing. He said he was. He told me he didn't see or hear anything, but he knew I saw and heard something. He said I had spoken in tongues.

I asked him to tell me first what he was laughing about. He told me he had gotten a phone call and letter that day from his former wife saying she was going to come to his town. He had sensed in his spirit that the devil who was operating through her had been dealt with, and by faith he could see him running. I told him I had actually seen him. That was what we were both laughing about, so we were agreeing in the Spirit.

I'm glad the devil is a defeated foe. *Jesus told me later that one doesn't have to have discerning of spirits to deal with the devil.* You may have it, but you don't have to have it. Some have thought they should wait to receive this gift from God. But He said you don't have to have discerning of spirits or be a minister to exercise authority over the devil. Every believer has the authority to use the Name of Jesus. Even the person who may feel he is the least member of the Body of Christ has that same right to use Jesus' Name. Jesus said anytime a person in or outside the Church is living in such a way as to intimidate, hinder, embarrass, or retard the ministry of the Church, you can know it is an evil spirit. We are supposed to deal with that spirit. The trouble is we try to deal with people, and that can get us in a mess.

You see, we can't exercise authority over people out-

side the Body of Christ, but we *can* deal with the spirit
that's operating there. I asked Jesus how to do that. He
said that in the privacy of your own prayer closet you
should say, "You foul spirit that's operating in the life of
So-and-so, hindering and embarrassing this church, I command you to desist in your maneuvers."

I was preaching along these lines in a Full Gospel
church in California and the pastor told me a year later
that he had three different families in his congregation who
had given him a lot of trouble. He knew after I preached
that it was the devil causing the trouble. One of the people
was his Sunday School superintendent and another was
a board member.

In the privacy of his own study, the pastor simply took
authority over the spirits causing the trouble, and com-
manded them to stop in their maneuvers right then. He
said it worked so smoothly it almost scared him.

He had been having trouble with these people three
years, but overnight they became his staunchest backers.
They had been trying to take money away from him, but
now they suggested he get more pay. He said the church
was better off than it had ever been. More money was coming in and more people were getting saved. More were getting filled with the Spirit.

I'm convinced we have more authority than we've ever
used. But instead of rising up and using what's ours, we
are too often prone to drift along, hoping things will get
better someday. Thank God for the Name of Jesus, now
and forevermore, and for the victory He already won for
us over the powers of darkness.